ART PRESERVES

What Can't Be Saved

Poems by

Carolyn Dahl

Copyright © 2019 Carolyn Dahl

All rights reserved. Except for brief quotations in critical reviews, this book, or parts thereof, must not be reproduced in any form without permission of the publisher or author. For further information or to order additional copies contact **The Orchard Street Press.**

ISBN: 978-0-9995826-7-1

Editor: John P. Kristofco

Cover Art: "Substitution" by John Slaby (johnslaby.com)
Author Photo: Thomas Perry

Printed in The United States of America by Bookmasters, Ashland, Ohio

Poem Credit: Quoted lines in "A Tiny Cup of Dreams" are from Ichinomiya Kii and Hachijo-in Takadura, *The Thirty-Six Immortal Women Poets*, translator Andrew Pekarik, George Braziller: New York, 1991.

The Orchard Street Press
P.O. Box 280
Gates Mills, Ohio 44040
330-264-7733
Orchard721@gmail.com
orchpress.com

Acknowledgments

My gratitude to the editors of the following publications in which some of these poems appeared:

ARTlines2: Art Becomes Poetry, Public Poetry & Museum of Fine Arts Houston: "Art Preserves What Can't Be Saved," winner of the grand prize.

Bearing the Mask: Southwestern Persona Poems, Dos Gatos Press: "Sweetie" and "I Give What Art Demands."

Civilized Beasts Vol. II, Weasel Press: "Why Do They Run."

Echoes of the Cordillera, Museum of Big Bend: "Destiny of Ice."

Goodbye, Mexico, Texas Review Press: "All Night Bus," "At a Luxury Resort," and "Parrots of Puerto Vallarta."

Poems About Music, Poetry Box: "Tree Top Tenor."

Rock & Sling 11.2, Whitworth University: "Rock-a-Bye."

Untameable City, Mutabilis Press: "Christmas in a Snowless City."

Public Poetry, On-Line: "To My Understudy," finalist award.

Special thanks to John Kristofco, publisher of The Orchard Street Press who became a friend during the production process; to Thomas Perry for technical assistance and constant support; and to many friends who lend their encouragement daily.

CONTENTS

WHAT ART DEMANDS
    Art Preserves What Can't Be Saved   1
    I Give What Art Demands   3
    His Father's Homely Sister-In-Law   4
    Sakura Bloom In Kyoto: Post-Tsunami   6
    Destiny Of Ice   7
    The Fine Art Of Suspension   8
    The Artist's Eyes   10
    Young Artist At An Exhibition   11

BRING A HEART
    Sweetie   13
    At A Luxury Resort   15
    The Parrots Of Puerto Vallarta   16
    Why Do They Run   17
    Tree Top Tenor   19

CARRY THEM HOME
    All Night Bus: Mexico   21
    Peihong's Good Life   23
    Milk Carton Girl   24
    Sleepless In My Mother's House   25
    In A City Garden   27
    Christmas In A Snowless City   28
    To My Understudy   29

IMMORTAL POET
    Rock-A-Bye   31
    First Date: Emily And An Admirer   33
    A Tiny Cup Of Dreams   35
    Immortal Poet   36
    When Your Poems Are Published   38

WHAT ART DEMANDS

✳ ✳ ✳

Art Preserves What Can't Be Saved
Coastal Scene with Shipping and Cattle:
Thomas Gainsborough

One cow separates herself from the herd,
stretches her neck, too far if you grew up
hugging cows. She stands on a cliff,
which our timid, clumsy animals would
never do, and points her horns toward
incoming ships. This is a fictional cow,
artifice from a painter's brush, yet the way
she lifts her head, smells the sea air, seems
real, as if she thinks she's come to the end
of fences, senses a reward of salt.

Once I sailed away on the broad back of a pet cow
brown as this one. We were unpartable shadows,
inventing our shapes in the summer creek,
splashing through ripples of tadpoles, pushing
against the current, believing we were going
somewhere, but eventually flowing back home,
happy and wet as the newly-hatched frogs
singing from the tip of her dripping tail.

Under the museum lights, the cow vanishes
in the glare of varnish as if its thinly painted
body needed to escape from the intensity
of eyes. My cow never returned from the dark
barn of profit. How I miss the weight of her
on our land. I thought she would always be there
like a childhood dress I imagine I can still wear.

I left the calm mythology of farms, never expected
to see her again, safe in a gold frame. Other people
pass by quickly. It's only a painting of a cow
and clouds, nothing they need to reclaim. I should
move on too. The guard is growing uneasy. He
doesn't know this is my memory pinned to the wall,
that I am riding the warm back of a sweet cow,
coaxing her down the dangerous cliff to the edge
of the painting where we jump the frame's fence.

I Give What Art Demands
For Artist Vance Kirkland

Each morning, I slip my body into straps
swinging from my studio's ceiling. The first
supports my chest, another cups the waist,
a third cradles thighs, the last lifts ankles into air.

I dangle above the canvas like a horizontal
astronaut of art flying in the room's sky, my back
illuminated by the hot suns of studio lights.

I practice the rhythm of suspension.
One hand, fingertips touched to canvas,
steadies my pendulum body. My other hand
grasps a wooden dowel dipped in color
to dot a spotted nebula into being.

Blood rushes, blushes, and sings
in my hanging head. Fumes rise
from the oil paint, sear my lungs
like inhaled comets. My muscles
cramp as the moon rolls over
the skylight, asks how long
can an angel fly obsessed
with beauty and celestial mind.

It's the angle of my body to the art
that reveals the image's truth.
To paint the desert, I lie in the sand.
To paint mountains, I climb their sides.
To paint the distant cosmos, I must lift
from earth, rise, hover like a star.

His Father's Homely Sister-In-Law
Mademoiselle Boissiere Knitting:
Gustave Caillebotte

The label writer
    judged her *homely*,
    weighting the painting with bias.

Maybe she would agree:
    her slack face unhooked from conversation,
    a large lip protruding, her face pale with age.
    She appears innocent, without guile,
    but did she know the blur of needles
    would attract a painter's eyes,
    that he would pause in the doorway,
    notice how the black of her dress
    enlivened the wallpaper flowers,
    startled the jade green of the chair,
    made everything gain beauty by association?

Maybe she understood
    a painter grows tired of the monotony
    of perfection, the demands of beautiful
    women for unerring depiction, and offered
    her plainness as a place to rest,
    to tinker with fallen standards.

They say if you study
    a painting, you can find the spot
    where the artist fell in love with the art.
    Her skin is dabbed with pinks, yellows,
    a touch of turquoise under the chin,
    a slice of lavender in the fold of her cheek.
    The artist played here, blessed her forehead
    with light as if he painted her thinking.

What does she think
>　of immortality now, her needles
>　forever clicking in a sound we almost hear?
>　Is there triumph in her downcast eyes?

She never returns our stares,
>　but allows us to enter her room,
>　watch her knit what we can't distinguish
>　in the soft light. The painter saw something
>　worthy in her to record. Maybe he believed
>　homeliness was a kind of clever beauty.

Sakura Bloom In Kyoto: Post-Tsunami

Hardly anyone comes to admire. Maybe
people aren't ready for trees adorned like pretty
                              geishas, limbs
overdressed for sorrow. Maybe they prefer
boney trees, not blossoms, or stunted branches,
                              bonsai, a crippled
beauty they could water with a spoon.

Maybe they question the value of beauty,
memories of picnics, sake and mochi. They
                              have no kitchens.
Blossoms are an inedible form of cherries.
Nothing they need after the earth shook,
                              waves roared.
Who would want to be near, or under anything

that falls now, even soft petals? They know
the sounds of falling walls, buildings,
                              the breaking
of family tea bowls kept safe for centuries.
What they can't hear is the sound of blossoms
                              opening.
Endings often look like beginnings.

Dying trees bloom wildly to ensure a seed's life.
Why should they trust a pretty tree's abundance?
                              Better to believe
in spiny coral lying on the ocean's floor, branches
working their tree-like roots around broken dishes
                              holding, binding
painted flowers together in a mended beauty.

Destiny Of Ice
Matanuska Glacier:
Photo by Jim Bones

The red tongues of volcanoes
  speak harshly to the sky.
    Plumes of ash rise,
      dry the perspiration
        of the sun, scar
          the purity of your skin
            with burning basalt veins.

Glacier, great white hump
  crawling down the mountain's muscle,
    you seem eternal. Dinosaur bones
      have slid under your belly, fossils sleep
        in the blue beds of your ancient ice,
          captured boulders scratch lines on chalk
            cliffs. Still, you are a fragile collector.

Your body, snow squeezed to ice,
  must fear a destiny of disappearing.
    When mountains cough scalding rain,
    when winter arrives timid as a rabbit,
    when suicide snowflakes refuse to fall
      with cosmic dust, will you starve, shrink,
      lacking the cold meat of winter?

Perhaps it will be a graceful end.
  Your spine slipping. Your body leaking
    streams of diminishment. Some calamities
    make no sound. The ligaments of crystals
    dissolve without cries. Alphabet islands
      linger silently, but their strange scripts
        spell a question: Is melting a loss,
        nourishment, or wild warning?

The Fine Art Of Suspension
*Hebe Watering Zeus Eagle:
Johann Baptist Lampi*

A night shadow,
bold and fringed,
crosses the moon.
Tamed by gravity,
an eagle lands
on a woman's wrist,
the flesh on her arm
tender and tearable
in beak and claws,
if the bird so wished.

The artist knows
terrestrial touch is not
a raptor's domain,
so one wing, the span
of nightmares, stays raised,
curved behind bare shoulders
like a pinioned collar.

She could lift her arm,
clip feathers, render it
flightless, if she chose.
But she has called this sky
god down, offered it a reason
to bend its sickle beak
to her bowl when the night
was bright for hunting.

In my backyard,
I offer songbirds simple seeds,
but uninvited, a hawk arrives
to feast on fragile wings.
It patrols the fence,
a sky terror with talons
that send the feeding sparrows
into the hedges to twitter in distress.

Eyes fixed as the moon,
fierce with hunger,
the hawk stares into
the tangle of branches
for shadows that might
flush into flight.

Is it my presence
that holds this moment safe,
keeps the hawk's claws locked
on the fence? I could change
the sparrows' fate if I desired.

And what holds an eagle
and this woman in
the assurance of
suspension? If
the painted moon
blinked out, the balance
of light shifted, would
the claw or the arm win?

The Artist's Eyes

St. Lucia, with your platter of eyes,
Can you roll her one like a marble?

Any color, or some of each will do.
She's only after light and sight

And the answer to *why* the insane
Mother can count every bead she wraps

Around her baby's neck to twist
The devil out of her corkscrew mind.

While an artist who lives for paint and color
Can barely see the tube she squeezes.

But spends her mornings with magazines
Ripping the eyes off pretty girls

To lay them softly over her own
As if she believed, St. Lucia could make

Paper eyes explode with sight.

Young Artist At An Exhibition

The cloth was soft,
sueded like calves' skin,
patterned with faint pink petals
scattered on a beige field. Sleeves
met her wrists, openwork crochet
decorated the bodice, and a skirt
flared to brush her new, ankle-
strapped, platform shoes.

The back neckline plunged
to the waist, uncovered the smooth
contours of a twenty-four-year-old
woman facing a canvas with friends,
lost in the artist's surreal world of paint.

She felt someone's stare
land on her bare back,
trace the pencil-fine edges
of shoulder blades,
drop into the charcoal
shadows of her spine,
measure the lighted swells
of moving muscles,
defining her without a face.

Curious, she turned into
the beam of sight.

An old man across the room,
white haired, body folded
like a broken toothpick,
sat next to a wife who engaged
his admirers, freeing his glittering
eyes to probe what he saw.

The young woman smiled.
In a gesture that would autograph
the moment forever in her mind,
she lifted her skirt, thrust out a shoe:
thick red square for a sole, tall purple
rectangle for a heel, black-and-white
stripes for the body: a Mondrian
composition strapped to her foot.

He nodded, then laughed
as she turned back to stunned friends
who couldn't believe she had stuck out
her foot to Max Ernst. How else could
she tell him? Her life too was ruled by art.

It was a kind of bow.

BRING A HEART

* * *

Sweetie

The spike buck raised its head, then ducked.
I hit the doe instead. Dressing her out, her belly

thumped under old coyote scars--they always
go for the softest part of their kill. I slit her open

gently and pulled out a kicking fawn, twirled it
round and round by its legs until the birth-juice

flew out of the lungs, off its long, blue tongue.
Wrapped in a horse blanket, it shivered, watched

me with eyes wet as gully washers as I loaded
the body of its mother into the truck. Wasn't

nothing to do but take them both home.
I called her Sweetie--she being a girl and all,

and liking sugar in her milk. I made a bottle
from a rubber glove, and she ate right well,

shooting up to the size of a calf. Frisky too.
She followed me to the arroyo, chased jack-

rabbits around the petroglyphs with the dogs,
licked my face every time I bent over anthills

to search their mounds for Indian beads
they always bring to the surface with sand.

When I went to town for supplies, Sweetie
rode in the pickup cab, head out the window

with the hounds. *Growing your own venison?*
the store clerks teased. *When's supper?*

Or, *You look like hell. New girlfriend
keeping you up all night?* Since Sweetie

came, I don't get a lick of sleep. When
the dogs sound off at night, I jump up

with my gun, fearing coyotes got a hold
of her. Tomorrow, I'm making her a bed

in the kitchen on Ma's old quilt so I get
some shut-eye. Yesterday, I worried

myself to the bottom of a whiskey bottle
fearing she'd run off and get herself shot.

Today, I made her a necklace from Indian
beads to mark her as a pet, not meat.

Sure as hell wish that spike buck hadn't ducked.

At A Luxury Resort

In a mini-zoo one night
a caged jaguar screams
a sound unformed by tongue,
amplified by rib bellows,
pressed through iron bars
until it shatters my tourist sleep,
brings me to the animal's side.

Once jaguars slid silently through
this jungle, spots rippling tall grass
vertical as swords. Their cries echoed
nine times in temples bearing their names,
and priests bent in fear and gratitude
offering sacrificial hearts to holy jaws.

What can I know of a caged god's needs?
The intrusion of my eyes breaks his patience,
sends him in circles on Nopalli-sized paws
to scratch scars in gray concrete. He
bellows again from his grassless cell,
sprays, as if at any moment he might
ignite, burn in his own water, and ascend.

The hotel believes he is a charm
on our vacation bracelets, exotic
to watch as a museum piece, eyes
studded with jade. But alone
at his dark cage, far from hotel lights,
real eyes warn me away. I'm not
the one he's calling. But tonight,
I'm the one who answers, the one
who remembers to bring him a heart.

The Parrots Of Puerto Vallarta

Midnight. We chattering tourists,
tamale-filled and Dos-Equis soaked,
wake the caged birds who make
drowsy attempts to answer,
tuck curved beaks under
iridescent wings, close their eyes,
fall away into a lost sky.

In the morning, I call them *macaws*,
the word *parrots* too melodious for shrieks
and squawks without a jungle chord
beneath them. I stand in a ring of droppings
that paint the concrete around their hotel cage
and apologize. I explain it is their beauty,
our lack of wings, makes us crazy to capture
and contain. Something in green feathers
we crave. Something in the flare of orange
above beaks that bewitches. They cock
their heads, listen eye to eye as if no one
had spoken gently to them before.

At the beach, teenagers parasail over
the Gulf, rise on fiesta-colored umbrellas
to claim the sky. These fledglings feel
the thrust of wind, see the planet's edge
curve, watch fish jump in the sun's glare.
They point their cameras at passing gulls,
then on themselves soaring in blue space.
Laughing and screaming, they are winched
back to earth, bodies aflame with flight
that burned away their words, left them
squealing and screeching on the sand.

Why Do They Run

Nostrils wide in elation, the horses'
chests heave under the stirruped legs
of mini-men who flash their stables'

silks in the sun and lurch over the speeding
animals like crayons scribbling color.
The horses' hooves slash the track, throw

dirt into the four-beat gait of the gaining
animal known to the lead by its breath,
foam flying from bit-laced mouths.

These are no gentle rocking horses,
but lineages bred to one desire: to run.
Sometimes the jockeys love them, whisper

into their ears, pat their muscled necks
before the summons to mount is called.
Mostly, the horses are "the talent," booked

by the jockey's agent for a two-minute
embrace, a forty-mile-an-hour love affair,
a hell-bent ride on a beast with frail ankles.

The race's winner becomes our Pegasus.
With mint juleps in hand, intoxicated
with luck, we believe we are two-minute gods.

When the jockey raises the trophy,
when red roses drape the exhausted horse,
the color matching the blood seeping

into its stressed lungs, we believe
in the myth we have made. But who will
hold the horse tonight, caress its muzzle,

lead it home the way Bedouins bring
their prize horses into tents, sleep next
to them, the honor theirs?

They know a horse
can outrun its heart. And it is
heart that makes a horse run.

Tree Top Tenor

Singing his arias from the top
of a red bud tree like a tenor
hoping to shatter glass, I unplug
my earphones and listen to his
mockingbird riff of blue jay,
cardinal, woodpecker stutter.

The way he struts his songs,
though hawks circle nearby,
makes me wonder: when
did I lose the courage to sing?

I remember warbling in front
of an old piano, plinking the ivories,
pumping my lungs to *Natural Woman,*
delirious with notes and reasons to sing.

When did I grow silent, believe music
no longer requires a throat?
The gray bird doesn't peck an app,
nor download the Top Ten Avian Tunes,
though he is a napster of birds' songs.

When he rewinds his song book
memory and without changing
feathers, trills an oriole, I shape
my soft lips to the point of a beak,
find my voice behind my teeth,
and scat-sing with the bird.

My husband rushes from
the house, binoculars dangling
from his neck and searches
the tree for a strange new bird
he has never heard.

Carry Them Home

✳ ✳ ✳

All Night Bus: Mexico

With a push and shove,
I board the dirty, dented bus.
It lurches forward, jerks
the roof riders clutching
racks and bleating goats.

In a seat for two, three of us squeeze.

Sandwiched in the middle, I press
against the aisle sitter's body, half
of which balances on a sliver of seat,
the other half suspends over the air
of the aisle, held in place by the push
of another body from across the gap.

Caught in a bridge, the two men
levitate like magicians over the abyss,
conjuring seats where none exist.

Daylight disappears into smudges,
flares briefly in fractured window cracks,
confusing the rooster who crows
beneath a man's serape. Sometimes
we skid to a stop in the desert's nowhere,
drop a family into shadows, their goat
leading the way home through
starlight and scorpions.

Shouldn't I be afraid? Saguaros rise
from the dark, thick arms raised like bandits
who might be real. I am a woman alone,
know no Spanish, riding with strangers
and a driver who is high on peyote,
in a rickety bus leaking carbon monoxide.

Yet, what I feel is peace.

I trust the dusty Madonna pasted
to the bus wall, her hand raised
in perpetual blessing. I find comfort
in fussing babies under mothers' rebozos,
smelling tortillas, the soft breaths
of the aisle sitter whose head
has nodded onto my shoulder.

I have the luxury of choice.

Yet, I chose this box of souls
rattling over rock-studded roads
on patched tires and rusted
axles. I don't sleep, but watch
the driver's rosary swing
from the broken mirror.
I hold my place in this moment
like the aisle sitters hold each other
over the abyss until morning.

Peihong's Good Life

I born in Peoples Republic of China
on small farm. I not study hard in school.
        Have no skills.
My future in my small village was bad.
So I think to go big city and work.

Man come who arrange good jobs
in the West. Snakehead say it complicated.
        Cost $40,000.
He say my parents pay part now. I pay later
when work. I send home money. We live good life.

My parents think it bring lucky future for me
and them. They give their savings to Snakehead.
        I promise to repay parents
from my job, my good salary. The man smile.
We all happy. I give him photos for passport.

In Shanghai, I given new clothes. Fly to Africa,
Amsterdam. Must say I am political refugee.
        Sleep on dirty floor. No heat.
I tell them I change my mind. Want to go home.
They burn me with cigarettes. Lock me in box.

Two days no food. They give me sexy clothes.
I forced to practice how to make men happy.
        I never have.
They pass me around at parties. Say will cut off
my lips if I not smile. No money to send home.

Parents must call me bad daughter. Took
their money and left them poor. They must think
        I live good life, clothes, apartment.
That I have forgotten Chinese roots and respect.
I have no way to tell them. No good life.

Milk Carton Girl

Mother
I am not missing.
I am not lost.
Crow-like men stole me,
a shiny new ring to hide
in their nest of girls.

Mother
Don't look where trains drag graffiti
from town to town. Look for a pretty
house with blinds that never open
and sullen boys who mow the yard
but never fill the empty bird bath.

Mother
Watch for flocks of men, only men,
flying in and out of the house.
Their migrations distract neighbors
from the fluttering fingers wedged
between blind slats, signaling.

Mother
I miss my pink bedroom, the quilt
we made from old dresses, teddy
guarding the night stand. I want
to apologize to the dolls for shelving
them so early when I thought
I was too old to play.

Mother
If you are late and I am already gone,
look for me in the backyard. The flowers
will be strangely tall, their colors
bright as screams. Pick a large bouquet.
Hold it in your arms. Carry me home.

Sleepless In My Mother's House

The distant highway sounds like bees in a wall.
White geese fly over the house, shrieking
like pterodactyls splashing into the swollen creek.

There is too much moon in this room.

Oak tree shadows fall through the window,
sleep on the carpet,
their smallest branches twitching
like fish in my lap.
I sit on a white couch floating like an iceberg
in the cold light of the night.

Ten dolls watch me.

My mother posed them in frozen gestures.
One doll's rubber arm waves,
her smile lost in shadow
though two white teeth gleam.
Another, tiger-eyed, polyester hair shining,
stands against a pillow,
her hands hidden in her skirt
like the secrets my mother would never reveal.

Another has painted blue eyes.
Its body is as large as mine was at two,
as if my mother purchased a sibling for me,
the baby a widow couldn't have.
Its head is cracked ear to ear.
As a child I outlined it with fingernail polish
because I believed pain to be red.

Rilke hated dolls, their lack of strength,

their unshifting gaze, their wanting something
in their doll-souls that deadened his imagination.
They begged with sweetness he couldn't bear.
But what did a housebound mother need?
Did the dolls remind her of when she was young
with babies,
or did she want children that stayed,
a small audience of human shapes
to sit on the couch
and witness her passing days?

This room is too quiet.

I wish the grandfather clock,
silent for ten years,
would gong;
that my sister's wedding portrait,
the veil moon-whitened,
would speak;
and the figurine on the piano
would play the etudes I never mastered.
I wish the bats who moved into the walls
when she didn't return
would flutter like fairies.
Or the ducks in the painting behind me
would rise from their colored lake,
carry me through the dark glass
into the moonlight,
and away on the departing creek.

In A City Garden

Under the blossoming cherry trees,
two teenage boys slouch in leather jackets,
chains dangling from heavy pockets.
Their blonde hair glows nightclub blue
as if they partied all night, or wish they had.
Perhaps they are embarrassed to be caught
in this pretty scene, adorned as they are
with falling petals, for they glower
at the couple with stares so perfected
the woman smiles, remembering her son
practicing frowns in the bathroom mirror.

Above them, breaking the garden's rules
and their code of coolness, a third boy
climbs a tree with *awesome* this, *awesome*
that. He picks a sprig of blossoms, only
a small twig, no unkindness to the tree,
and slides down the trunk, shaking loose
a cloud of petals so dense only his earring
can be seen flashing gold like a bird's eye.

Do the blossoms have scent? The man asks.
The boy sniffs. *Not much.* The woman wants
to ask, not out of judgement but curiosity, if he
thinks the metal in his nose rings affects a sense
of smell the way her silver fillings taint the taste
of strawberries, but she stays silent. With a nod
to the couple, the boy joins the other two,
pelting them with petals as they swagger
away through drifts of fallen blossoms,
the pink in his pocket already fading like
the innocence indifference wants to erase.

Christmas In A Snowless City

Plywood snowmen, outlined in red,
shimmy in the wind, spook
the dogs on their nightly walks.
Sprouting hedges tinkle with plastic
icicles and electric candles flame
in my windows, but never burn curtains.

A spiky door garland, creamed with fiber
snow and sprayed with pine scent, welcomes
a disheveled man who offers to paint
my address on the curb. "So your relations
won't get lost." He pauses, sniffs the air.
"Reminds me of cuttin' spruce with my Pa.
Snow thigh-high. Those trees cried all
the way home on the sled. I'd pick sap tears
from the snow. Chew 'em like bitter gum."

I give him the $25 because his mention
of snow makes him a type of relative
from my Christmas card past. With
the whiskey breath of a favorite uncle,
he whispers, "I can't git the spirit here.
Not without snow." I slip him another $10.

I'm ready to invite him inside for chocolate,
a stray gift, a discussion of the virtues
of snow, but he pulls out his stencils
and spray cans and shuffles down the drive
to glitter the curb for relatives who won't
be coming. The paint can hisses. His face
flares briefly in the glow-in-the-dark color.
"Who can believe in snow angels
made of green grass.....anyhow."

To My Understudy

Tonight, I want to hush the deafening applause

> for you, my understudy,
> who always believed
> in the possibility
> of my impending disasters:
> the wobbly trapdoor,
> the frayed light cords,
> flu-carrying kisses,
> off-stage breakdowns.

You spent months waiting to fly from dim wings

> into dumbfounding radiance
> to replace me, the fallen star.
> Perhaps you served the play's
> artifice well, rendered my lines
> with grace. Though you didn't cause
> the misfortune that thrust you into
> the animating light, you are still
> a thief of roles, an embezzler of words.

Do not mistake understanding for permission.

> I own the sorrows of this stage,
> the colors of the painted scrim sky.
> My body scents the cloth of costumes.
> Theatre ghosts cry in my voice all night.
> The rubber knife measures the length
> of my fingers and will plunge only
> into my believing heart.

Tomorrow, the peacock returns.

> With feathered eyes I'll watch
> the sparrow retreat to obscurity,
> a caged bird who has seen the sun,
> but must wait for ill winds to soar again.
> When the curtain rises, it will be me
> stepping out of myself into the burn
> of another life, the heat of clapping hands.

Never again will you steal my illusions.

> One single moment
> in this pretend world
> is the whole life
> I was meant to live.

Immortal Poet

* * *

Rock-A-Bye

        Each morning I sit in her rocker,
diminutive chair for women five feet,
        or a little above,
nervous types, who even at rest
        move forward and backward.

        Surrounded by books,
coffee in her China cup,
        I dream into the outer space
of imagination. I write poems
        about wolves with red stripes,
frogs with transparent lungs,
        butterflies tied to swallows.
"Things to keep your mind busy,"
        she used to say.

        Now when she calls,
she wants to go home
        to where she really lives,
has filled her cavernous wheelchair
        with rhinestone jewelry,
crochet hooks, her mother's silver,
        a clean blouse for church,
and Hummel figurines
        of children forever kissing.

       She begs me to come,
help her move the oak bed frame
       she no longer owns.
Outside her window,
       she says strangers without faces
are burying rabbits in the flower bed,
       space ships are blasting toy men
to the moon, shaking her bathroom
       and breaking her hip.

       Every morning she steals bacon
from the cafeteria, hides it
       between her knees
for the tabby cat who wandered
       out of her father's cornfield.
Only she can see it. Locked in her wheelchair,
       she rocks back and forth,
stroking her cat into existence.
       A mind needs something to keep it busy.

First Date: Emily And An Admirer

The restaurant roars like buffalos breaking
free of nickels. Though the room is flambe
hot, their tongues stick to iced glasses,
and conversation labors as if air
has to be borrowed from libraries.

    Emily says:
I am one who failed for beauty.
My life is unopened on the shelf.
    He replies:
I will write my name on every page,
erase the sentences that toil.

She blushes like the Duck a l'Orange,
lying naked on a bed of wild rice, dreaming
backwards to its eggshell summer.
Glazed with migratory envy, it endures
the probes of their forks that love only lips.

    She looks away:
My days are weighted with all the bees
of the clover well.
    He says:
I will collect them in daffodils.
A thing with feathers will sing you
specimens of song.

    She protests:
But I have a funeral in my brain!
    He counters:
I have a cage that catches
the slant of light that oppresses.

The Bananas Foster arrives, the waiter ignites
the liquor, the flames flare and hiss, the sugar
carmelizes and grows brittle from neglect.

    She looks down:
Eve's sweet apple
was the first forbidden dessert.
    He smiles:
Ecstasy is always paid for with anguish.

    She smoothes her hair:
Your words are sweeping away my heart
with many colored brooms.
    He moves closer:
For you,
I would dust the pond with rainbows.

In the mirrored serving spoon,
they watch their reflections
cling to opposite rims,
slip on the butter smear,
slide into the spoon's bowl
and touch.

    She whispers:
But can you find the key to my heart
hidden inside a fainting robin?
    He says:
I have hummingbirds
whose beaks leave no scars.

Her body ripples, grows limp
as the peach halves the waiter slips
into their red wine, the bubbles
rising like hundreds of hindered rubies.

A Tiny Cup Of Dreams

When I drink sake   the geisha on the blue
bottle begins   to undulate   in layers
of patterned kimonos   I peel off
the label   frame it in gold   because
             I want to be her

Lonely geisha   dressed for love   hair starched
with rice water   kimono pulled back   from
the nape   of the neck   the spot men love
to kiss   You could be   an immortal poet
                honored
in ancient times   holding an inked   brush
made from   your own   black hair   stroking
a love poem   onto pale   mulberry paper
in letters   soft as silk scarves   draped
                over bamboo leaves

A small cup   of sake   warms   her lips
She hears rising waves   "their cries in the night"
The room's   paper screens are open   Moths circle
her brush   She bends to the table   pushes back
                ink-dyed sleeves
to write   one more poem   before moonlight
disappears   She imagines "in the moon   the face
of the one   she loves"   How the years   stretch
like thread   in summer   yet the tangle of love
             will not be cut

Sake is   the broom   that sweeps   away
sadness   the hook to catch   shy poems
a dream that dreams   worlds Who could say
I am not   the face   painted   on the label?
             All portraits are imaginary

Immortal Poet

Some nights, I think I am Japanese
and compose poems in imperfect
romaji script with a fude
made from my dog's hair:

koe wa uta desu
keredomo hanashite yo
kaze wa fukumasu
tsubane haru ni nakimasu

Then I send them to prestigious publications
signing Tatsu Yume, my pen name,
which means Dragon Dream.
Most Japanese poets write incognito,
signing poems with haiku-like phrases.
Given names are sufficient for daily life,
but not the moment of inspiration
when it is said: "Poets' eyes flare with fire,
and they fly from one world to the next
on the backs of dragons, trailing poems
behind them like dusky smoke."

Sometimes an editor responds:

Dear Tatsu Yume:
Please send translations.
ASAP!

Dragon Dream replies:

Could a lichen-covered rock
decipher its own effaced surface?
Though I lie in bed
all the flower-filled morning,
though my tears water
the plum trees on my kimono,
though I sit in a bamboo grove
until my senses heighten,
I cannot regain
the language of intoxication.
These poems waved at me
from the tips of the catalpa tree.
High on sake or verse,
I cannot translate the veins of leaves.

The Editor E-mails:

Dear Author:
May your hair tangle with words.
May your book's cover fade.
May you be forced to eat live centipedes
from Central Park and sell your poems
from a beggar's bowl on Eighth Avenue.

Sincerely, The New York Times.

When Your Poems Are Published

Shouldn't

Italian seraphim   sing   ethereal harmonies
fireworks whoosh   umbrella-blossom your house
horns bleat-sweet in the street   sirens whoop-whoop
clouds arrange   a whipped-cream   exaltation

Shouldn't

your mother call   claim   you rhymed words
with pablum   your   father admit   poems may save
lives   as well as scalpels   friends treat you to lunch
forgive neglect   fill the empty spaces   departed
poems left   with champagne   carbonated bubbles
fizzing in your brain   like new poems trying to form

Shouldn't

your publisher   send candy grams   cavorting clowns
in wigs   and bobble-headed announcers   interrupt
the Rose Bowl   to recite your poems   as if something
amazing   had been won   or Twitter tweets proclaim
blogs buzz with critics' praise   Flickr fans post photos
Vimeo videos   show you waving from   a red convertible
tossing book   order forms   to literate crowds

Shouldn't

your lover read   each poem slowly to you   in bed at
night   letting the words   return   to your body
taste of stanzas   flush of rhyme   stroke of verbs
nuzzle of metaphors   until   you're not sure   if
they are   your poems   or your lover's   body

Shouldn't

the book glow   at night   resting   on the bedside
stand   luminescent night light   born of your
mind's darkness   shining   beyond your world
pages moving   hand   to   hand   turning
like stars   crossing   the limitless horizon

Shouldn't

the Earth wobble   even a degree   and molecules
make space   when poems   alight   and
cling   to the world's   gyrating song?

Carolyn Dahl was the grand prize winner in the national 2015 ARTlines2 poetry contest, a finalist in the PEN Texas Literary competition in nonfiction, and the 2018 Malovrh-Fenlon Poetry Prize. Her essays and poems have been published in twenty-six anthologies including *Women On Poetry* (McFarland), *Goodbye, Mexico* (Texas Review Press), *Beyond Forgetting* (Kent State), and in various literary journals, including: *Copper Nickel, Plainsongs, Rock & Sling, Camas,* and *Hawaii Review.* She is co-author of the poetry and art book *The Painted Door Opened.*

Also a visual artist, Carolyn has shown her work in museums and national galleries. She has been a guest artist on HGTV and PBS, authored three art books: *Transforming Fabric I&II* (F&W Books) and *Natural Impressions* (Watson-Guptill). When she isn't writing or making art, Carolyn raises monarch butterflies in her kitchen and sets them free in her Houston garden.
www.carolyndahlstudio.com